A Special Gift

For

_____

From

_____

Date

_____

Message

_____

_____

COME INTO HIS LIGHT

Catherine Marshall

COME INTO HIS LIGHT
by Catherine Marshall

© 1995 by Leonard E. LeSourd

Originally published under the title *Day by Day with Catherine Marshall* by Chosen Books, a division of Baker Book House Company, Grand Rapids, Michigan, 49516, U.S.A.

© 1995: Christian Art, P.O. Box 1599, Vereeniging, South Africa

Designed by: Christian Art

ISBN 0-8007-7150-8

© All rights reserved.

Our God is the Divine Alchemist. He can take junk from the rubbish heap of life, and melting this base refuse in the pure fire of His love, hand us back – gold.

He knows the way I take; when He has tried me, I shall come forth as gold.
Job 23:10

Like a great bell tolling over all the land, the consistent voice of the sovereign power of God reverberates throughout Old Testament and New. He is omnipotent, omnipresent, omniscient in this life and the next. We cannot believe this and also think that our God is no match for the evil of the world.

"Do I not fill the heavens and the earth?" declares the Lord.
Jeremiah 23:24

The Gospel truly is good news. The news is that there is no situation – no breakage, no loss, no grief, no sin, no mess – so dreadful that out of it God cannot bring good, total good, not just "spiritual" good, if we will allow Him to.

*I am like a luxuriant cypress;
from Me comes your fruit.
Hosea 14:8*

Any human physician requires the surrender of a given case into his care; he can do nothing unless the patient agrees to follow his orders. Common sense told me that exactly the same was true of the Great Physician.

"And why do you call Me, 'Lord, Lord,' and do not do what I say?"
Luke 6:46

"John is a great man, the greatest," Jesus was saying. Yet the humblest disciple in the Kingdom has riches and privileges and authority of which John never dreamed. How could that be? Because man's efforts were at an end. In the new era of the Kingdom it would be God's Spirit *in* man doing the work.

"Seek first His kingdom and His righteousness."
Matthew 6:33

God insists that we ask, not because He needs to know our situation, but because *we* need the spiritual discipline of asking.

"Ask, and it shall be given to you."
Matthew 7:7

The reason many of us retreat into vague generalities when we pray is not because we think too highly of God, but because we think too little.

"For I, the Lord, do not change."
Malachi 3:6

In order to make sure that we are not retreating from the tension of faith, it is helpful to ask ourselves as we pray, "Do I really expect anything to happen?" This will prevent us from going window-shopping in prayer.

Jesus said to the centurion, "Go your way; let it be done to you as you have believed."
Matthew 8:13

Because God loves us so much, He often guides us by planting His own lovely dream in the barren soil of a human heart. When the dream has matured, and the time for its fulfillment is ripe, to our astonishment and delight, we find that God's will has become our will, and our will, God's.

... according to the kind intention of His will.
Ephesians 1:5

Jesus' humor was always for a purpose. Sometimes it was His bridge to an individual He would otherwise have had trouble reaching. Most often it was to illuminate a truth.

"You blind guides, who strain out a gnat and swallow a camel!"
Matthew 23:24

To awaken people at every level of their being, Jesus used every weapon of language and communication to achieve His goals; most effective were the humorous thrusts and banter about those who put on airs. Jesus sees all our incongruities and absurdities, and He laughs along with us.

"For it is easier for a camel to go through the eye of a needle, than for a rich man to enter the kingdom of God."
Luke 18:25

Jesus spoke often of heaven's rewards. If that offends us by seeming too materialistic, perhaps we should be wary of being more "spiritual" than our Lord.

"And your reward will be great."
Luke 6:35

I guessed that this meant that the one who has stepped over into the next life still remembers every tender moment on earth, still cares what happens to those left behind, still wants to help them – but that the emotion of his love is intensified and purified.

For in the resurrection they ...
are like angels in heaven.
Matthew 22:30

We have the apostle Paul, in his famous love poem, setting love at the summit of all spiritual gifts, describing for us in gladsome detail what it will be like someday. It was on this conception of a new kind of love, on a different kind of relationship that I had to fix my mind.

Love never fails.
1 Corinthians 13:8

Often God has to shut a door in our face so that He can subsequently open the door through which He wants us to go.

We are the people of His pasture, and the sheep of His hand.
Psalm 95:7

My Teacher had yet to show me the difference between the presumption that masquerades as faith and real faith. The dividing line between the two lies at the point of one's motive.

He will bring me out to the light, and I will see His righteousness.
Micah 7:9

Jesus delighted in comparing earthly fathers to His heavenly Father, and then in adding, "But how much more God!" The riches of heaven and earth all belong to our Father, and He loves to shower them upon us. In Jesus' eyes though, the most precious of all gifts is this one of the Holy Spirit.

"How much more shall your heavenly Father give the Holy Spirit to those who ask Him?"
Luke 11:13

God deals differently with each of us. He knows no "typical" case. He seeks us out at a point in our own need and runs down the road to meet us. This individualized treatment should delight rather than confuse us, because it so clearly reveals the highly personal quality of God's love and concern.

"His father saw him ... and ran and embraced him."
Luke 15:20

Jesus' ringing response leaves no doubt: "I do choose. Be cleansed." And Jesus is the portrait of God. By every word and deed, Jesus made it clear that His Father not only cares, but that no detail of any life is too insignificant for His loving providence.

"And he who beholds Me beholds the One who sent Me."
John 12:45

As I read through the Gospels I see that Jesus had quite a bit to say about joy. We are not invited to a relationship that will take away our fun but asked to "enter into the joy of the Lord." The purpose of His coming to earth, Jesus said, was in order that our joy might be full!

[God] hath anointed Thee
with the oil of gladness.
Hebrews 1:9

I can see that Jesus drew men and women into the Kingdom by promising them two things: first trouble – hardship, danger; and second, joy. But what curious alchemy is this that He can make even danger and hardship seem joyous?

"In the world you have tribulation, but take courage; I have overcome the world."
John 16:33

It is wise to give God a chance to speak to us each day, perhaps the first thing in the morning when the mind is freshest. A few minutes of quietness help us focus on the areas where we most need God's help.

In the morning, O Lord, Thou wilt hear my voice; in the morning I will order my prayer to Thee and eagerly watch.
Psalm 5:3

Jesus stands sentinel over His Book to show us that we can use His word in Scripture with real power only as He Himself energizes it and speaks to us personally through it.

All things came into being through Him; and apart from Him nothing came into being that has come into being.
John 1:3

God cannot get His word through to us when our prayers are limited to self-centered monologues.

"For whoever wishes to save his life shall lose it; but whoever loses his life for My sake shall find it."
Matthew 16:25

By saturating my mind with Bible verses I find that the grayness lifts, the spirit is infused with spiritual food and I am ready to meet any difficulty that comes along.

[Jesus] entered the synagogue on the Sabbath, and stood up to read. And the book of the prophet Isaiah was handed to Him.
Luke 4:16-17

Until we catch a glimpse of the full glory of this crowned Christ, of the honors heaped upon Him, of the extent of the power the Father has placed in His hands, we can never grasp the significance of Jesus' question, "Who do you say that I am?" For Christ is the King of kings and the Lord of lords.

"When He ascended on high, He led captive a host of captives."
Ephesians 4:8

My first discovery was that I knew almost nothing about praise. The subject is mentioned occasionally as a nice worship exercise, a sort of icing on the cake as a gesture to God, but praise as the key to answered prayer, no. That was a new concept altogether.

At that time Jesus answered and said, "I praise Thee, O Father, Lord of heaven and earth."
Matthew 11:25

The quickest way to go to meet Him is through praise. No wonder we meet Him there, for Scripture goes on to teach us that God actually "inhabits" (lives in) the praises of His people.

Yet Thou art holy, O Thou who art enthroned upon the praises of Israel.
Psalm 22:3

The fact that the word "sacrifice" is used regarding praise tells us that the writers of Scripture understood well that when we praise God for trouble, we're giving up something. What we're sacrificing is the right to the blessings we think are due to us.

Through Him then, let us continually offer up a sacrifice of praise to God.
Hebrews 13:15

Even as God asked praise of Jehoshaphat and of Paul and Silas, so He asks it of each one of us. And the longer one ponders this matter of praise and experiments with it, the more evidence comes to light that here is the most powerful prayer of all, a golden bridge to the heart of God.

*Thou art my God, and I
give thanks to Thee.
Psalm 118:28*

He is always Light, so I too must walk in the light. All closed doors, every shuttered room in me must be thrown open. So began months of soul searching.

And every one who has this hope fixed on Him purifies himself, just as He is pure.
1 John 3:3

I wanted authoritative answers. Therefore, I went directly to the most authoritative source I knew – the Scriptures. And I discovered what I should have known before – that when you and I go to the Bible out of great need to learn what it has to say to us, it is then that we get real help.

Thy word is a lamp to my feet.
Psalm 119:105

God, who created heaven and earth, will hear *my* voice? The King of the universe will consider *my* meditation? Oh, thank You, Lord, for the undreamed-of opportunity of this audience with the King!

Worship the Lord with reverence, and rejoice with trembling.
Psalm 2:11

Faith is not hocus-pocus, opposed to knowledge and reality. In fact, faith does not go against experience at all; rather it appeals to experience, just as science does. The difference is that it appeals to experience in a realm where our five senses are not supreme rulers.

Now faith is ... the conviction of things not seen.
Hebrews 11:1

Faith is strengthened only as we ourselves exercise it. We have to apply it to our problems: poverty, bodily ills, bereavement, job troubles, tangled human relationships.

By faith Moses, when he was born, was hidden for three months by his parents, because they saw he was a beautiful child; and they were not afraid of the king's edict.
Hebrews 11:23

We cannot have faith and a guilty conscience at the same time. Every time faith will fade away.

"To give His people the knowledge of salvation by the forgiveness of their sins, because of the tender mercy of our God ..."
Luke 1:77-78

Faith has to be in the present tense – now. A vague prospect that what we want will transpire in the future is not faith, but hope.

"Blessed is she who believed that there would be a fulfillment of what had been spoken to her by the Lord."
Luke 1:43-45

Each of us is infinitely precious in the Father's sight, so much so that He knows every detail about us, even to the number of hairs on our heads.

"Look at the birds of the air, that they do not sow ... and yet your heavenly Father feeds them. Are you not worth much more than they?"
Matthew 6:26

Faith means that we must let Him do the work. Almost always it takes longer than we think it should. When we grow impatient and try a deliverance of our own, through friends or circumstances, we are taking God's work out of His hands.

The Lord is our lawgiver, the Lord is our king; He will save us.
Isaiah 33:22

Once I thought that faith was believing this or that specific thing in my mind with never a doubt. Now I know that faith is nothing more or less than actively trusting God.

"Do you believe that I am able to do this?"
Matthew 9:28

The idea that He might have a particular purpose for any one of us – a reason why we are here on earth – boggles the mind. So as He begins to unfold that bigger design into which we fit, it is up to us to take the first step forward in obedience.

And the Lord said to him, "Arise and go to the street called Straight."
Acts 9:11

The psalmist says that when he is hemmed in on every side, the Lord frees him. Gradually I have learned to recognize this hemming-in as one of God's most loving devices for teaching us that He is real and gloriously adequate for our problems.

But know that the Lord has set apart the godly man for Himself; the Lord hears when I call to Him.
Psalm 4:3

Nor can trust ever end in just intellectual faith or lip service to faith. When it is the real thing, it will spill over into action – and that will mean obedience.

*As a result of the works,
faith was perfected.*
James 2:22

How can we *not* want to obey when we begin to comprehend the magnitude of the Holy Spirit's love and complete good will for us?

For it is God who is at work in you, both to will and to work for His good pleasure.
Philippians 2:13

I knew that anything unloving in me, any resentment, unforgiveness or impurity would shut out God, just as a muddy windowpane obscures the sunlight.

Let us keep living by that same standard to which we have attained.
Philippians 3:16

Here we have Jesus telling us that convicting one another is not, and never was, our work: It's the Holy Spirit's business. Each of us must receive illumination about his guilt from the inside.

And he said, "Who art Thou, Lord?" And He said, "I am Jesus whom you are persecuting."
Acts 9:5

Long ago we had learned the principle that it is necessary to get the past confessed and straightened out (as far as is possible) before we can live abundantly in the present.

And if he has committed sins, they will be forgiven him.
James 5:15

If I truly believe that I am a child of a King, then my fear will disappear. Worrying would be the sure sign that I did not believe God's ownership of earth's resources. To think myself a pauper is to deny either the King's riches or my being His beloved child.

*The earth is the Lord's,
and all it contains.
Psalm 24:1*

There's no way to get our world back together again except as each of us begins with himself and with his own family.

"Just as the Father has loved me, I have also loved you; abide in My love."
John 15:9

F ear is like a screen erected between us and God so that His power cannot get through to us.

The Lord is the defense of my life; whom shall I dread?
Psalm 27:1

Sometimes it helps to write down one's fears, then hold them up one by one to the light of Christ's clear understanding. Never is Jesus as the Light of the world more clear than in these murky areas of our semiconscious fears, most of them unreal and psychotic.

Thou hast removed all the wicked of the earth like dross; therefore I love Thy testimonies.
Psalm 119:119

The time came when I realized that, in Jesus' eyes, fear is a sin since it is acting out a lack of trust in God.

"Why are you troubled, and why do doubts arise in your hearts?"
Luke 24:38

Faith is the strong tower into which we can run for protection today. It isn't a physical place but the light of a protecting Presence. It makes the unreal fears vanish and gives us literal protection against the real ones.

"And there is no other God and a Savior; there is none except Me."
Isaiah 45:21

Sometimes life finds us powerless before facts that cannot be changed. Then we can only stand still at the bottom of the pit and claim for our particular trouble that best of all promises, that God will make even this to "work together for good."

What then shall we say to these things? If God is for us, who is against us?
Romans 8:31

Why would God insist on helplessness as a prerequisite to answered prayer? One obvious reason is because our human helplessness is bedrock fact. God is a realist and insists that we be realists too.

"For the Lord God is my strength and song, and He has become my salvation."
Psalm 12:2

It should not surprise us that creativity arises out of the pit of life rather than the high places. For creativity is the ability to put old material into new form. And it is only when old molds are broken up by need or suffering, compelling us to regroup, that the creative process starts to flow.

"Call to Me, and I will answer you, and I will tell you great and mighty things, which you do not know."
Jeremiah 33:3

The secret of receiving is to give – even out of poverty. In fact, the more sunk we are in visions of lack, the greater need we have to start giving.

"There is a lad here, who has five barley loaves, and two fish, but what are these for so many people?" Jesus said, "Have the people sit down."
John 6:9-10

We shall be able to remember, to think, to will, to love, to worship and to understand so much more on the other side of the barrier of death. Our new life will be no sleeping, non-conscious or unfeeling existence.

"In my Father's house are many dwelling places; if it were not so, I would have told you."
John 14:2

Christ's words to the dying thief would have been nonsense had He not meant that after death on that very day, both He and the thief would know themselves to be themselves, would remember that they had suffered together, would recognize each other.

"Truly I say to you, today you shall be with Me in Paradise."
Luke 23:43

Scripture makes it clear that Jesus Himself is the only One who can baptize us with the Spirit. That is why there must always be the first step of commitment to Jesus (being "born again") before we can receive the fullness of His Spirit.

"This is the one who baptizes in the Holy Spirit."
John 1:33

The way to win out when I feel evil at work in my life and the lives of those I love is not to fight it in the ordinary sense, but to give over those I love completely into the Father's hands, knowing that I am helpless to cope with evil, but that He is able.

"Do not resist him who is evil."
Matthew 5:39

The unforgettable truth of David's Psalm 23 came alive in my experience: "He *maketh* me to lie down in green pastures" – thus sometimes using illness to get our full attention.

The Lord is my shepherd.
Psalm 23:1

So long as we are deluding ourselves that human resources can supply our heart's desires, we are believing a lie. And it is impossible for prayers to be answered out of a foundation of self-deception and untruth.

Examine yourselves!
2 Corinthians 13:5

God is not going to drop into our laps, as a package commodity, unselfishness or a loving disposition or any virtue. Instead, He has promised me Jesus' resurrection life in me. Thus it will be Jesus' selflessness and patience and love manifested in my life – not my own.

In Him you have been made complete, and He is the head over all rule and authority.
Colossians 2:10

Reading through the journals of my college years makes me aware as never before how tender God was with me, never intruding on my willful self-centeredness, but always there when the heart hungers inside me cried out.

Great is Thy faithfulness.
Lamentations 3:23

Jesus told His disciples to tarry until they received the Holy Spirit's power to become His witnesses. Note that Jesus did not say that this gift is for our own spiritual development or perfection or happiness. All of those results will follow provided we accept Jesus' top priority – witnessing to the world.

"For even the Son of Man did not come to be served, but to serve."
Mark 10:45

Apparently the surrender of self is necessary groundwork for receiving guidance, since not even God can lead us until we want to be led. It is as if we are given an inner receiving set at birth, but the set is not tuned in until we actively turn our lives over to God.

"O Lord, be Thou my helper."
Psalm 30:10

Most of us think of our lives in compartments – home life, business life, social life. Actually the various aspects of a truly creative life must dovetail. God will not direct a man's business life, for example, when the man insists on running his family life his own way.

"For where your treasure is, there will your heart be also."
Matthew 6:21

In seeking guidance, I discovered that it was important to concentrate on one or two questions on which I needed light, and ask God for directions on those. This selectivity proved more effective than trying to make my mind blank, ready to receive any message on any subject.

Commit your works to the Lord, and your plans will be established.
Proverbs 16:3

One reason the first Christians received so much guidance was that they had *koinonia*, a corporate fellowship that made them "of one heart and soul." It was in this setting that illumination, inspiration and guidance flourished.

*These all with one mind
were continually devoting
themselves to prayer.
Acts 1:14*

Then there is the check of providential circumstances. We are most fortunate in having this test. When we have asked God to guide us, we have to accept by faith the fact that He is doing so. This means that when He closes a door in our faces, we do well not to try to crash that door.

"He who is holy, who is true, ... who opens and no one will shut, and who shuts and no one opens ..."
Revelation 3:7

I found in the matter of guidance that I had to be willing to obey – no matter what. Otherwise no directions would be forthcoming. Receiving guidance is definitely not a matter of telling God what we want and hoping that He will approve.

The mind of a man plans his way, but the Lord directs his steps.
Proverbs 16:9

I have found that the inner Voice is more likely to speak to me at the first moment of consciousness upon awakening, or during some odd moment of the day as I go about routine tasks, than while I wait expectantly with pad and pencil in hand.

"Sanctify them in the truth; Thy word is truth."
John 17:17

So far as the virtues and graces we need for victory in our lives – faith, joy, patience, peace of mind, the ability to love the wretched and the unlovely – there is no way we can work up such qualities. Paul tells us that these are gifts of the Holy Spirit. They can be had in no other way.

Pursue love, yet desire earnestly spiritual gifts.
1 Corinthians 14:1

Are we ready to give ourselves to others? He will accept no excuses about our inadequacy in this way or that. Giving us adequacy is His business. That's what His coming to us is all about.

Whoever wishes to become great among you shall be your servant.
Mark 10:43

Jesus had told me what to do. At that moment I understood as never before the totality of His respect for the free will He has given us and the fact that He will *never* violate it. His attitude said, "The decision is entirely yours."

And He said to them, "What do you want Me to do for you?"
Mark 10:36

We want salvation from our sins and we yearn for eternal life. We think that we can earn these things. Then we find out, as Paul did, that we cannot pile up enough good marks and merits to earn anything from God. No, salvation "is the gift of God; not as a result of works, that no one should boast."

For by grace you have been saved through faith; and ... not as a result of works.
Ephesians 2:8-9

Sometime in life every one of us finds himself out of control, caught in circumstances that he is helpless to change. We are to welcome such times. Often it is only then that we lesser spirits enter into the truth of Jesus' statement from the fifteenth chapter of John: "Apart from Me you can do nothing."

"Apart from me you can do nothing."
John 15:5

Certainly there is enormous pressure on all of us to be accepted and approved by others. But God wants us to resist this pressure. Consider the tragedy of the religious leaders of Jesus' day.

For they loved the approval of men rather than the approval of God.
John 12:43

In order to fly we must have two wings. One wing is the realization of our human helplessness, the other is the realization of God's power. Our faith in God's ability to handle our particular situation is the connecting link.

Be renewed in the spirit of your mind.
Ephesians 4:23

Fellowship with Jesus is the true purpose of life and the only foundation for eternity. It is real, this daily fellowship He offers us.

"Abide in Me, and I in you."
John 15:4

For each of us – no matter what our situation or how we feel we have failed – there is hope.

I will wait for the Lord ... I will even look eagerly for Him.
Isaiah 8:17

We are told that in our daily task – whatever our vocation or profession or daily round – we are to seek to please God more than man.

Whatever you do, do your work heartily, as for the Lord rather than for men.
Colossians 3:23

As for whether God means for us to include material needs in our petitions, certainly Christ was interested in men's bodies as well as their souls. He was concerned about their diseases, their physical hunger. Christianity, almost alone among world religions, acknowledges material things as real and important.

Your heavenly Father knows that you need all these things.
Matthew 6:32

God does not want our obedience out of fear. Our obedience to Him is the fruit of lives growing in the rich soil of love and trust. Our obedience is to be at once both the result of our loving God and also the proof of our love.

"Thy will be done, on earth as it is in heaven."
Matthew 6:10

But what exactly are we to obey? Since Jesus often mentioned His commandments, I found it helpful to read the Gospels through, setting down in a notebook the commandments that Christ Himself gave us. There are a remarkable number of them and many are surprisingly precise.

"I did not come to abolish [the Law], but to fulfill [it]."
Matthew 5:17

Not one of us is going to drop his fishing nets, leave all and go after Jesus – unless he feels he can trust Him. One memorable sentence quoted by Quakeress Hannah Smith sums it up: "Perfect obedience would be perfect happiness if only we had perfect confidence in the power we were obeying."

And when they saw Him, they worshiped Him.
Matthew 28:17

Sometimes even as I would open my mouth to speak, there would be a sharp check on the inside. I soon learned that the Holy Spirit sought to prevent careless words or critical words or even too many words. Nor would He tolerate even a trace of sarcasm, or faithless words of doubt or fear.

When He, the Spirit of truth, comes, He will guide you into all the truth.
John 16:13

Jesus was simply stating a law of life when He told us, "Judge and you will be judged." Put this way, judging others constantly cultivates more soil for the thistles of fear-of-man to grow in.

"For in the way you judge, you will be judged."
Matthew 7:2

God asks that we worship Him with concentrated minds as well as allowing the Spirit to direct our wills and emotions. A divided and scattered mind is not at its most receptive.

And their eyes were opened and they recognized Him.
Luke 24:32

I found that in the everydayness of life when the inner guidance did not obviously violate any of God's loving laws or hurt another, it was important to obey and thus experiment with obedience. That was how I learned to recognize the Holy Spirit's voice.

"And I will make all My mountains a road, and My highways will be raised up."
Isaiah 49:11

Scripture piles reassurance upon reassurance that at the death of the physical body, the real person inside lives on without interruption. The Bible tells us that the next life is not only a fully conscious one with every intellectual and spiritual faculty intact but that these faculties are heightened.

Then I shall know fully just as I also have been fully known.
1 Corinthians 13:12

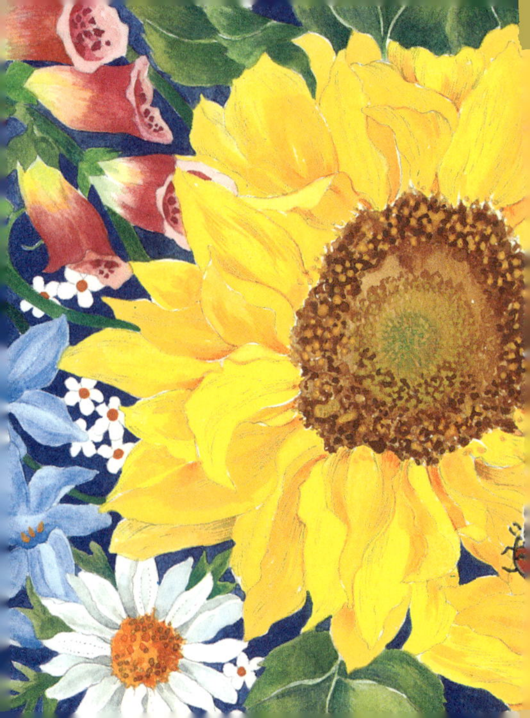